TABLE OF CONTENTS

1 INTRODUCTION

People generally do not spend a lot of time thinking about the weather, unless, of course, it is going to affect some type of activity. If you are planning a picnic, a sunny day is probably more desirable than a day filled with thunderstorms. If you are a farmer, a few days of steady rain might be what you are hoping for. Whatever you may be looking for, weather and climate probably don't seem the most exciting of topics. The fact is, however, that weather and climate affect our day-to-day lives in ways that most people do not consider.

Our many different types of weather and climate affect the type and amount of food we grow. Weather and climate affect how easily we can transport food and other products to markets all over the world. They also affect the decisions we make about where to live and how we use Earth's resources for energy.

▼ Weather conditions can include gray skies, hail, and a rainbow all at the same time.

GARETH ST
VITAL SCIENCE
Earth Science

AIR AND WEATHER

by Barbara Davis
Science curriculum consultant: Suzy Gazlay, M.A.,
science curriculum resource teacher

Gareth Stevens
Publishing

Please visit our web site at: www.garethstevens.com
For a free color catalog describing Gareth Stevens Publishing's
list of high-quality books and multimedia programs, call
1-800-542-2595 (USA) or 1-800-387-3178 (Canada).
Gareth Stevens Publishing's fax: (877) 542-2596

Library of Congress Cataloging-in-Publication Data

Davis, Barbara J.
   Air and weather / Barbara J. Davis.
      p. cm. — (Gareth Stevens vital science - earth science)
   Includes bibliographical references and index.
   ISBN-13: 978-0-8368-7760-1 (lib. bdg.)
   ISBN-13: 978-0-8368-7871-4 (softcover)
   1. Weather—Juvenile literature. 2. Air—Juvenile literature. I. Title.
QC981.3.D387   2007
551.6—dc22   2006033112

This edition first published in 2007 by
Gareth Stevens Publishing
A Weekly Reader Company
1 Reader's Digest Rd.
Pleasantville, NY 10570-7000 USA

Produced by White-Thomson Publishing Ltd.
Editor: Clare Collinson
Designer: Clare Nicholas
Photo researcher/commissioning editor: Stephen White-Thomson
Gareth Stevens editorial direction: Mark Sachner
Gareth Stevens editor: Leifa Butrick
Gareth Stevens art direction: Tammy West
Gareth Stevens production: Jessica Yanke and Robert Kraus

Science curriculum consultant: Tom Lough, Ph.D., Associate Professor of Science Education,
Murray State University, Murray, Kentucky

Illustrations by Peter Bull Art Studio
Photo credits: CORBIS, pp. 4 (© Tim Wimborne/Reuters), 8 (© Nawang Sherpa/Bogati/ZUMA), cover and
28 (© Eric Nguyen/Jim Reed Photography), 35 (© Jim Sugar), 36 (© John Maier Jr/Argus Fotoarchiv/
Corbis Sygma); Ecoscene, p. 43; ©iStockphoto.com pp. 5, 6, 10 (Robert Brown), 14 (Joe Gough),
18 (Michal Koziarski), 19l (Paul Prescott), 19r (Ulrike Hammerich), 20 (Manfred Gehrke), 22
(Mark Clarkson), 23 (Dainis Derics), title page and 27 (Moritz von Hacht), 30 (Michael Braun),
32 (Doug Webb), 33 (Eric Bechtold), 40 (Martin Kawalski), 41 ((both), 42 (Alex Timaios),
45l (Paulus Rusyanto), 45r (Frank Pitthan); NASA, p. 31.

Cover: This violent tornado was one of several that occurred in south central Texas in June 2004. Tornadoes
are more common in the United States than anywhere else in the world.
Title page: Lightning bolts strike a city at night, illuminating the skyline. Lightning contains a huge amount
of electrical energy that is strong enough to kill people and animals.

Printed in the United States of America

2 3 4 5 6 7 8 9 10 10 09 08

From microscopic bacteria to the largest tree or animal, every organism on Earth is affected by the climate in which it lives. Climate is one of the most important factors affecting the number and types of organisms that can live in any particular area.

What Is Weather?

Weather describes the conditions in Earth's atmosphere at any time or over a short period of time. Weather conditions include the temperature of the air, the speed of the wind, and the amount of water in the air (humidity). In many places on Earth, the weather changes daily.

What Is Climate?

The typical, long-term weather pattern in a particular area is known as its climate. Climates vary greatly in different parts of the world. The United States has the most varied climate of any country on Earth. There are polar regions in Alaska, where the temperature is extremely low and few plants can grow. There are tropical areas in Hawaii and Florida, where it is hot all year round. Just as weather changes from day to day, Earth's climate can change, but this happens slowly, usually over tens, hundreds, or thousands of years.

▲ Lightning brightens a desert's night sky. Weather often changes very quickly.

This book explores the composition of Earth's atmosphere, its layers, and its characteristics. It explains how wind is created by differences in air temperature and air pressure and how these factors affect types of winds and wind patterns around the world. This book also describes clouds, thunderstorms, tornadoes, and hurricanes and examines how the ways in which we choose to live might affect the relationship between Earth's atmosphere, weather, and climate.

2 EARTH'S ATMOSPHERE

Earth is surrounded by a blanket of mixed gases called the atmosphere. The atmosphere is extremely important to all of us because without it there would be no life on Earth. The mixture of gases that make up Earth's atmosphere is commonly known as air. The atmosphere stops Earth from becoming too hot or too cold. It traps enough of the Sun's heat energy to warm Earth's surface. At the same time, it shields Earth from the Sun's harmful radiation. The atmosphere is held in place by gravity, a force that attracts things to Earth.

Atmospheric Gases

About 99 percent of Earth's atmosphere is made up of nitrogen and oxygen gases. The remaining 1 percent is made up of argon and traces of other gases such as carbon dioxide, methane, and water vapor. Although they are only present in tiny amounts, carbon dioxide and methane are important because they absorb heat energy given off from Earth. Without these gases, heat would be lost

▲ In this photo taken from outer space, Earth's atmosphere can be seen as a layer of mixed gases surrounding the planet.

into space, and life would not be able to exist on Earth. In addition to the mixed gases, the remaining 1 percent of Earth's atmosphere includes traces of solid particles such as ice crystals, salt crystals, dust particles, and pollen.

The atmosphere contains about 78 percent nitrogen and 21 percent oxygen. The amount of other gases in Earth's

Gases in Earth's Atmosphere

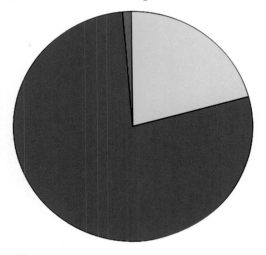

- ■ Nitrogen 78%
- □ Oxygen 21%
- ■ Other gases and particles 1%

▲ Most of Earth's atmosphere is made up of nitrogen and oxygen gas. There are also very small amounts of other gases.

atmosphere, however, varies slightly from season to season and from place to place. For example, as much as 5 percent of the air above a tropical rain forest may be water vapor. In the middle of Death Valley, California, the amount of water vapor in the air may drop to zero. There is likely to be more carbon dioxide gas in the air above a large city than there is in the air above a smaller city. This is because burning fossil fuels such as coal and oil releases extra carbon dioxide into the air. In a larger city there are probably more factories and people driving cars, so more fossil fuel is being burned.

Air Density

You have probably heard the phrase "lighter than air." It suggests that the air that forms Earth's atmosphere has no substance at all. The fact is air is made up of molecules and atoms of gas. The molecules and atoms have mass, so therefore air has mass. Air also has density.

The more molecules there are in a certain amount of air, the greater the density of the air. Air density is affected by altitude. The higher up in Earth's atmosphere you travel, the less dense the air. This is why it is harder to breathe at high altitudes. As you go higher, the oxygen molecules in the air become fewer and farther between, so you get less oxygen with every breath you take.

Atmospheric Pressure

Pressure is the amount of force pushing on an area. Atmospheric pressure is the force exerted by the weight of the air pressing down on the surface of Earth. Atmospheric pressure is greatest nearest Earth's surface. This is because the air is most dense nearest Earth's surface. At sea level, air is pushing down with a

▲ The air is less dense at the top of a mountain. There are fewer oxygen molecules, making it harder to breathe.

force of 14.7 pounds per square inch (1.03 kilograms per square centimeter). Pressure decreases higher in the atmosphere because air density decreases. Atmospheric pressure varies from one place to another. Variations in atmospheric pressure play an important part in creating different weather conditions around the world, especially wind.

Layers of the Atmosphere

Earth's atmosphere is divided into four main layers: the troposphere, the stratosphere, the mesosphere, and the thermosphere. The pressure and temperature of the atmosphere change dramatically from layer to layer.

The Troposphere

The troposphere, or lower atmosphere, is the layer closest to Earth's surface. This is the layer in which we live. The layer gets its name from the Greek word *tropos*, which means "a turn" or "a change." Conditions in the troposphere are constantly changing, from place to place and from season to season. Almost all of Earth's weather, including wind, rain, and clouds, takes place in the troposphere.

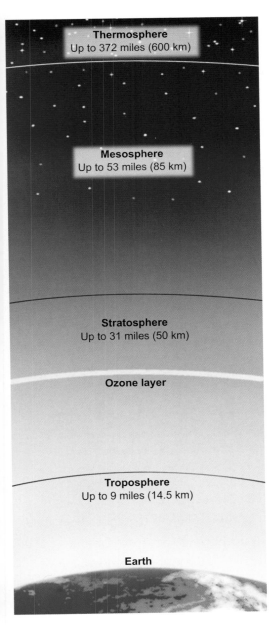

Thermosphere
Up to 372 miles (600 km)

Mesosphere
Up to 53 miles (85 km)

Stratosphere
Up to 31 miles (50 km)

Ozone layer

Troposphere
Up to 9 miles (14.5 km)

Earth

▲ Even though Earth's atmosphere has four layers, most of the gases are found in the troposphere.

The troposphere is the shallowest layer of the atmosphere. At the North and South Poles, the troposphere extends about 5 miles (8 kilometers) above Earth's surface. The layer gets deeper toward the equator, where it extends almost 9 miles (14.5 km). Although it is shallow, the troposphere contains about 80 percent of all the gases in the atmosphere. This means that the troposphere also has most of the atmosphere's mass.

Temperatures in the troposphere are highest near to Earth. This is because most of the heat in the troposphere comes from Earth's surface. The temperature rapidly decreases as you move up through the troposphere and away from Earth's surface. At the top of the troposphere, the temperature is an extremely cold –76° Fahrenheit (–60° Celsius).

The Stratosphere

The layer above the troposphere is called the stratosphere. The layer gets its name from the Latin word *stratus*, which means "a spreading out" or "a layer." The stratosphere begins at the top of the troposphere and extends to about 31 miles (50 km) above Earth's surface. The stratosphere contains about 19 percent of the gases in the atmosphere. Compared to the troposphere, the stratosphere contains

Exploring the Troposphere

In the nineteenth century, the air above Earth was a big mystery to most people. In every age, however, there are explorers whose curiosity leads them into the unknown. In 1804, a young French scientist named Joseph-Louis Gay-Lussac yearned to know more about the gases in Earth's atmosphere. At the time, the only way to explore the atmosphere was to take a dangerous trip in a big basket attached to an even bigger hydrogen balloon. Gay-Lussac and another scientist traveled more than 2 miles (3 km) up into the troposphere. Gay-Lussac made a second trip alone. This time, he traveled more than 4 miles (6 km) into the troposphere—higher than anyone had ever been before. Using a variety of instruments, Gay-Lussac measured the air temperature and pressure. He also took measurements of Earth's magnetism. The data he collected helped answer many questions about how temperature and other factors affect gases.

less water vapor and it is less dense. Because it is dry, the stratosphere has almost no clouds. Jet airplanes usually fly in the stratosphere to avoid the weather conditions in the troposphere.

The stratosphere is a particularly important layer because it contains ozone, a gas that absorbs the Sun's harmful radiation. Ozone in the stratosphere prevents the harmful radiation from reaching Earth. Unlike in the troposphere, the temperature in the stratosphere increases with height. This is because the stratosphere is heated by the Sun from above instead of by Earth from below. Ozone absorbs the Sun's energy as heat, trapping much of it in the upper portion of the stratosphere.

▲ When you fly in an airplane in the stratosphere, you can often see clouds in the troposphere below.

The Mesosphere

The mesosphere is the layer above the stratosphere. *Meso* means "middle." Together, the stratosphere and mesosphere are sometimes known as the middle atmosphere. The mesosphere begins about 31 miles (50 km) above Earth's surface and extends to 53 miles (85 km). Even though the mesosphere is closer to the Sun than the stratosphere, it is the coldest layer of the atmosphere. This is because most of the mesosphere contains few gases to absorb energy from the Sun. It is hottest at the bottom and gets colder with height. The outer edge of the mesosphere has temperatures as low as −130°F (−90°C). This is even lower than the lowest temperature ever recorded on Earth. It is cold enough to freeze water vapor into ice clouds, which can sometimes be seen at night.

The mesosphere protects Earth from being hit by stray chunks of rock and metal falling from space, called meteoroids. When meteoroids from space enter Earth's atmosphere, they become known as meteors. Have you ever seen a shooting star? Shooting stars are actually trails of gases that form when meteors burn up in the mesosphere.

The Thermosphere

The fourth main layer of Earth's atmosphere is called the thermosphere. This layer gets its name from the Greek word *thermes*, which means "heat." The thermosphere is sometimes known as the upper atmosphere. It begins 53 miles (85 km) above Earth's surface and extends about 372 miles (600 km). The gas molecules in the layer become farther and farther apart as you go up through the thermosphere and gradually blend with outer space. Space shuttles sometimes orbit Earth in the thermosphere.

Temperatures in the thermosphere increase with height. This is because, even though there are few gas molecules in the layer, the molecules absorb radiation from the Sun. The thermosphere has temperatures that can reach more than 3,000°F (1,700°C).

Energy in Earth's Atmosphere

Almost all of the energy that drives Earth's weather and climate comes from the Sun. This energy has both magnetic and electrical properties. It moves through space in the form of electromagnetic waves. The transfer of energy from the Sun to Earth's atmosphere is a type of electromagnetic radiation.

Earth receives only a very small amount of the electromagnetic radiation produced by the Sun. Even this tiny amount, however, is enough energy to power all the natural cycles that allow life to exist on Earth.

Not all places on Earth receive the same amount of the Sun's energy. If they did, temperatures all over the world would be more alike. The Sun's rays have the strongest effect around the equator, where they reach Earth's surface straight on. Farther away from the equator, the effect of the Sun's rays is weaker. This is because the rays do not reach Earth's surface so directly and the heat is spread out over a wider area.

As the rays of the Sun enter Earth's atmosphere, some are absorbed. Water vapor and carbon dioxide in the atmosphere absorb some types of radiation. Other gases, dust, and even clouds also absorb some of the Sun's energy. The ozone layer in the stratosphere absorbs harmful types of radiation. Earth's surface itself absorbs some energy, which helps heat the land and water. Earth's atmosphere and its surface absorb about 70 percent of the energy that reaches Earth's atmosphere. The remaining 30 percent is reflected back into space.

Have you ever seen a mirror reflect sunlight back into your eyes? Clouds can act in the same way. As the Sun's rays hit the clouds, some are reflected away from Earth. Dust particles and gas molecules can also reflect the Sun's rays.

▼ Gases, dust, and clouds in Earth's atmosphere absorb or reflect the Sun's rays.

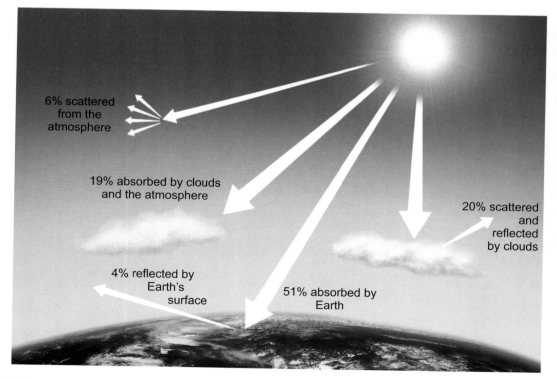

6% scattered from the atmosphere

19% absorbed by clouds and the atmosphere

20% scattered and reflected by clouds

4% reflected by Earth's surface

51% absorbed by Earth

3 INFLUENCES ON WEATHER

Earth's weather is influenced by three main factors: the temperature of the air, the movement of air caused by differences in atmospheric pressure, and the amount of water in the air.

Changes in Air Temperature

As you know, Earth's weather takes place in the troposphere. You also know that temperature decreases as you travel up through the troposphere. This happens because Earth's warm surface heats the troposphere. Earth's surface absorbs some of the Sun's energy and then transfers it back out. Much of this energy is transferred by a process called convection. Convection is the transfer of heat energy through movement of a liquid or gas. As the molecules in the liquid or gas move, any heat the molecules have absorbed moves with them.

Air rises or sinks depending on its temperature. Warm air rises. Cold air sinks. It sinks because cold air is denser than warm air. The constant rising and sinking of warm and cold air can create a continuous movement of air called a convection current.

Throughout the day, Earth's surface absorbs energy from the Sun and becomes warmer than the air. The warm surface of Earth heats up the air molecules close to the surface. As you know, when air temperature increases, the air becomes less dense. The cooler, denser air above it pushes down and moves the warmer air up. This convection current

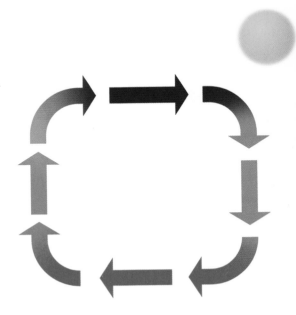

▲ The blue arrows show how cool air pushes down on the warmer air (the red arrows), which then rises. This constant activity is called a convection current.

is repeated over and over again. This is how heat moves through the troposphere.

The Sun's rays hit Earth most directly over the equator, so it is in this region that the air temperature is highest. At the North and South Poles, the Sun's energy is spread out over a larger area, so temperatures are lower. This results in huge convection currents in the atmosphere, as air moves from cooler areas, where the air is more dense, to warmer areas, where the air is less dense.

Changes in Atmospheric Pressure

Along with temperature, the pressure of the air in the troposphere also changes. When warm air rises, the air becomes less dense. As the air density is lowered, so is the atmospheric pressure. When cold air sinks, it increases the air density and the atmospheric pressure. The cold air flows under the warm air, causing warm air to rise. Because the Sun's rays do not reach all regions of the world straight on, they do not heat up the world evenly. This means there are constant changes in atmospheric pressure around the world. The gases in our atmosphere respond to these changes by moving. They move from higher pressure areas to lower pressure areas. If it is a horizontal, or side-to-side, movement, the result is wind.

Winds

Winds are caused by the movement of air, resulting from differences in air temperature and atmospheric pressure around the world. There are several different types of wind, but all winds blow from areas where the atmospheric pressure is high toward areas where the atmospheric pressure is low.

Winds are described by the direction and speed in which they travel. You have probably heard the phrase "the cold North wind." This is a wind that starts

▲ Weather vanes have been used for centuries to show the direction from which the wind is blowing. Usually, the arrow at the top of the weather vane points into the wind. For example, if the arrow lines up exactly with the letter *W*, it means that the wind is blowing from the west.

in the north and blows south. You may hear weather forecasters mention "south-easterly" or "northeasterly" winds. This simply describes winds moving from the south or north but also moving a little east at the same time. The wind that blows most frequently in a particular region is known as a prevailing wind.

Local Winds

Winds are also described by the size of the area over which they blow. Local winds blow over short distances. Like all winds, local winds are caused by differences in air temperature and atmospheric pressure, which result in the movement of air from an area of high pressure to an area of low pressure.

A breeze from a small inland lake would be an example of a local wind. During the day, the land absorbs the Sun's heat more quickly than the lake's water does. The land reflects back some of this heat energy into the air above it. The warm air over the land rises, creating a low-pressure area. Cooler air from over the water moves in to replace the warm air. Since the wind is coming from over the water, it is called a lake breeze. At night, the opposite happens. The land cools off more quickly than the water in the lake. The cooler air above the land

moves out to replace the warmer air over the lake. Because the wind is moving from the land out over the water, it is known as a land breeze.

Global Winds

Global winds blow from certain directions and travel over long distances. Like all winds, global winds are caused by differences in air temperature and atmospheric pressure over Earth's surface. The cold air at the North and South Poles is denser than the warm air around the equator, so the atmospheric pressure is high. This causes wind at Earth's surface to blow from the poles toward the lower pressure area around the equator. At the equator, warm air rises. As it rises higher in the atmosphere, it cools and travels toward the poles. The winds blowing from the poles toward the equator and from the equator toward the poles are global winds.

The Coriolis Effect

Because Earth is spinning, global winds do not blow directly from north to south or south to north. The rotation of Earth causes winds to swerve sideways. North of the equator, the winds blowing toward the North Pole gradually swerve northeast. The winds blowing south toward the equator gradually swerve southwest. South of the equator, the winds blowing toward the South Pole swerve southeast and the winds blowing north toward the equator swerve northwest. The swerve in the winds caused by Earth's rotation is called the Coriolis effect.

Wind Belts

The trade winds are the winds blowing toward the equator from the northeast above the equator and from the southeast below it. They are called the trade winds because sailors depended on them to fill the sails of the trading ships that carried goods across the ocean from Europe to South America and the West Indies.

Trade winds blowing toward the equator from the south and the north meet at the equator. The winds rise as they are heated, so there are no steady surface winds at the equator. This area is known as the doldrums. Sailors dreaded the doldrums because there was no wind to fill the ships' sails. A ship could spend weeks floating on the sea without making any real progress.

The winds that blow toward the poles between 30 degrees and 60 degrees latitude are called the prevailing westerlies. These winds originate in the west but seem to bend toward the east. Polar

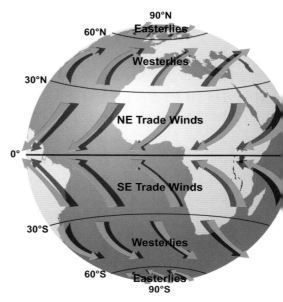

▲ Global winds swerve as they travel around Earth because of the Coriolis effect. Some areas are very calm, with hardly any wind at all. Other areas have belts of steady winds.

easterlies form over the poles when the atmosphere cools. As the air flows away from the poles, it swerves toward the west because of the Coriolis effect.

Water in the Air

Earth's water is constantly being recycled between Earth, the atmosphere, and living things. This never-ending movement of water between Earth's surface, the atmosphere, and living things is called the water cycle.

Water vapor enters the atmosphere from oceans, lakes, and other bodies of water through a process called evaporation. Evaporation takes place when water

High Winds and Wind Chills

A nice cool breeze might feel wonderful on a hot summer day. That same breeze may not feel so pleasant on a cold day in winter. This is because wind blowing over your skin takes away body heat. The stronger the wind, the cooler you feel. This effect is called the wind-chill factor. Weather forecasters calculate the wind-chill factor to let you know how the combination of cold temperatures and strong winds can act to take away heat from your body. For example, a temperature of 25°F (−4°C) combined with winds that are blowing at 30 miles (48 km)per hour will act on your bare skin as if the temperature was −6°F (−21°C). That is cold enough to cause damage to bare skin in a very short time.

molecules escape into the air as water vapor, a gas. Water vapor also enters the air from plants and animals. Even water in the soil evaporates and passes into the air as water vapor.

As water vapor rises in the atmosphere, it cools and some of it condenses into droplets of liquid water. These water droplets gather together as clouds. As the water droplets grow larger, they fall back

Water Cycle

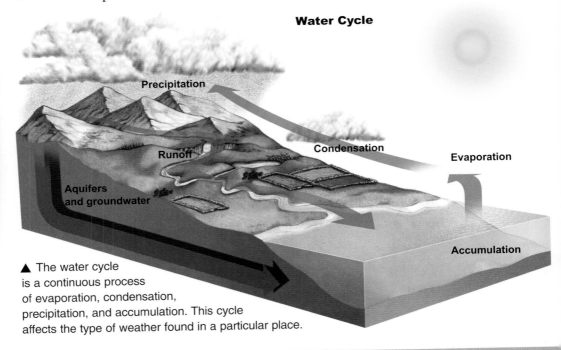

▲ The water cycle is a continuous process of evaporation, condensation, precipitation, and accumulation. This cycle affects the type of weather found in a particular place.

to Earth's surface in the form of precipitation. Precipitation includes rain, sleet, snow, hail, and fog. As part of the water cycle, some of the water from the precipitation will enter the atmosphere again as water vapor.

It's Not the Heat, It's the Humidity

Relative humidity is a common measurement. It compares the amount of water vapor in the air with the greatest amount of water vapor that it is possible for a certain amount of air to contain at a particular temperature. When the relative humidity is high, there is more water vapor in the air than when the relative humidity is low. You know that air or wind passing over your skin causes you to lose body heat. This happens because water vapor evaporates from your skin. This helps to keep you cool on a hot day. If the relative humidity is high, it becomes harder for the water to evaporate. You do not feel as cool. Relative humidity is expressed as a percentage. For example, the relative humidity in the dry Sahara desert is usually about 20–25 percent. In western Washington State the relative humidity is usually between 78 percent and 87 percent.

Clouds

Clouds are classified by their shapes and how high in the atmosphere they form. There are four main cloud classifications: cumulus, stratus, cirrus, and nimbus. Each type of cloud is linked to a particular type of weather. Knowing the meanings of each of these words will help you remember the types of clouds they describe. Combinations of these words are also used to describe a type of "combination" cloud.

The word *cumulus* comes from the Latin word for "pile" or "heap." To many people, that is exactly what a cumulus cloud looks like: a big heap of fluffy cotton balls. Cumulus clouds

▼ Fluffy cumulus clouds are often seen on dry, sunny days. They usually mean there is no rain in the weather forecast.

usually form fairly close to Earth's sur-face, about 1 mile (2 km) up in the air. Cumulus clouds are often associated with pleasant days and they usually mean that precipitation is unlikely.

Stratus clouds get their name from the Latin word for "a spreading out" or "a layer." It is the same word from which the word *stratosphere* comes. The name gives a good idea of what stratus clouds look like. Stratus clouds form low, flat layers that may seem to cover almost all of the sky. Stratus clouds may sometimes bring some damp drizzle, but they do not necessarily bring rain.

▲ Cirrus clouds are wispy and seem to drift high in the sky.

The word *cirrus* is taken from the Latin word for "curl of hair." Cirrus clouds are thin and feathery. They form high above Earth's surface where temperatures are very low. Because of this, cirrus clouds are made mainly of ice crystals. The presence of cirrus clouds does not mean bad weather is likely. If, however, a cirrus cloud looks as if it is combined with a cumulus cloud, thunderstorms may be on the way.

The word *nimbus* comes from the Latin word for "rain." Nimbus is used to

▲ Stratus clouds spread out like a gray blanket over the sky. The presence of stratus clouds usually means it will be a gloomy day.

describe clouds that produce rain or snow. Nimbus clouds are thick and often dark. They seem to hang heavy in the sky. These clouds usually form between 7,000 feet (2,100 meters) and 15,000 feet (4,600 m) above Earth's surface. The word nimbus is often combined with the names of other types of cloud to indicate a cloud that produces precipitation. For example, if a cumulus cloud becomes tall

▶ If a stratus cloud thickens and becomes dark gray, it becomes a nimbostratus cloud, a layered cloud that usually produces rain.

The Man Who Named the Clouds

All his life, Luke Howard loved studying weather and clouds. His cloud-watching hobby led him to develop a classification system. In 1802, Howard presented his detailed drawings and observations. At the time, scientists used Latin as the language of their scientific studies. Howard decided to do the same. He identified four classes of clouds. He believed that all cloud formations were either one of the four classes or a combination of one or more classes. Howard's names are still used by meteorologists today. Try putting together some of the names to create your own types of clouds. What type of weather would they announce?

Cloud Name	Meaning in Latin	Cloud Description
Cumulus	Heap or pile	Heaps or piles that build upward
Stratus	A spreading out or layer	Wide, blanketlike clouds
Cirrus	Curl of hair	Wispy curls of clouds that spread in all directions
Nimbus	Rain	Cloud system that is producing rain

and develops a flat top, it becomes a cumulonimbus cloud. Cumulonimbus clouds are heaps of clouds that produce rain and thunderstorms.

Fog

It may not be possible to walk on clouds, but if you live in an area that sees any kind of fog, you have probably walked through a cloud. Fog is a cloud that forms close to the ground. Most fog forms when the air's relative humidity reaches 100 percent at ground level. At this point the air is said to be saturated. The temperature at which the air becomes 100 percent saturated with water is called the dew point. When the air temperature reaches the dew point, water vapor in the air condenses into water droplets, which we see as fog. Fog forms most often when the ground cools at night, especially after a particularly warm and humid day.

Water from Clouds

Any form of water that falls to the ground from a cloud is called precipitation. In warm areas of the world, precipitation usually comes in the form of rain or drizzle. In cold temperatures, precipitation comes in forms such as hail, freezing rain, sleet, and snow.

Rain and Drizzle

What is the difference between rain and drizzle? Rain describes drops of water that are at least 0.02 inches (0.5 millimeters) in diameter. The drops are usually widely separated as they fall. Drops that are smaller than this, which fall close together, are called drizzle. Drizzle usually falls from stratus clouds.

Rainmakers

For as long as there have been farmers, there have been attempts to call up needed rain. No matter how hard people tried to make it rain, however, rainfall remained a matter of luck—until the 1940s, that is. In 1946, physics researcher Vincent Schaefer demonstrated a way to make rain. Schaefer's experiments showed that a grain of dry ice planted like a seed in an existing natural cloud formed millions of ice crystals. These crystals would fall to the ground in the form of precipitation.

A few years later, an atmospheric scientist named Bernard Vonnegut discovered that "planting" silver iodide in clouds made even more ice crystals. This method is still used by rainmaking companies around the world. The process is called "seeding" a cloud. The crop? Rain! The People's Republic of China now has the largest cloud seeding system in the modern world.

Freezing Rain and Sleet

Sometimes raindrops fall through cold air with a temperature of less than 32°F (0°C). This is the freezing point for water. When the raindrops fall through such cold air, they freeze into particles of ice. If the particles are smaller than 0.02 inches (0.5 mm), the precipitation is called sleet. Raindrops that do not freeze until they touch a cold surface are called freezing rain. Freezing rain can cause ice storms in which wires, telephone poles, and roadways become slick with layers of ice.

Hail

Hail describes balls of ice larger than 0.02 inches (0.5 mm). Each ball of ice, or hailstone, starts out as a small particle of ice inside a cold area of a cloud. Air movement inside the cloud moves the particle up and down. This movement causes the particle to pick up more and more layers of ice. When it is heavy

▼ Ice storms can occur when rain falls onto freezing-cold surfaces. When the drops of rainwater hit the cold surface, they freeze into a coating of solid ice.

enough, the hailstone falls to the ground. Sometimes, hailstones become quite large. The largest hailstone to have fallen in the United States measured almost 19 inches (48 cm) around (circumference). Some hailstones reach falling speeds of 100 miles (160 km) per hour. When large hailstones fall at a high speed they become very dangerous to animals, people, buildings, and vehicles.

▲ Snowflakes often melt and fall as rain, but when the air near the ground is cold enough, the snowflakes fall as snow.

Snow

Snow forms when water vapor in a cloud changes into ice crystals with six points. You see these crystals as snowflakes. It is rare to actually see one snowflake, though. Usually, they stick together as they fall from the sky.

4 WEATHER PATTERNS

One minute it is sunny, then within minutes it seems there is a storm moving in. Weather can change very quickly from day to day, sometimes from hour to hour. Major weather changes are caused by the movement of large amounts of air called air masses.

Air Masses

An air mass is exactly what it sounds like: a large body of air. An air mass can cover thousands of square miles. An air mass can also be more than 6 miles (10 km) high. Whatever size it is, each air mass is characterized by its own temperature range, level of humidity, and atmospheric pressure. Air masses are classified using two of these characteristics: temperature and humidity.

The temperature characteristics of an air mass are described as arctic (bitterly cold), polar (cold), or tropical (hot). The humidity characteristics are described as either continental or maritime. The word *continental* is used to describe air masses with low humidity. These air masses form over land. The word *maritime* is used to describe air masses with a higher level of water vapor. These air masses form over the oceans.

There are five main air masses that affect the weather in North America. Continental arctic air masses form over the far northern arctic regions. These air masses bring extremely cold, dry weather during winter. They may sweep across Canada, causing bitterly cold temperatures in central and eastern parts of the United States. Continental polar air masses form over Alaska and northern Canada, bringing weather that is dry and cold, but not as cold as that brought by continental arctic air masses.

Maritime polar air masses are cold and very moist. They form over the North Atlantic and North Pacific Oceans. Because the air masses carry so much water vapor, they bring rain, fog, and snow. Seattle, Washington, on the North American Pacific coast, receives some of the highest amounts of rain of any U.S. city. The city is in the path of a maritime polar air mass that sweeps in on a regular basis.

Hot, dry weather arrives with continental tropical air masses. These masses form during the summer over northern Mexico and the southwestern part of the United States. Think about what you have heard about the dry deserts of southwestern parts of the United States, such as those in Arizona, New Mexico, and West Texas. They are in the path of continental tropical air masses. Sometimes, these hot, dry air masses reach farther inland than usual. If they move into the Great Plains region of North America, they can cause long periods of drier weather than usual.

Maritime tropical air masses bring hot, moist weather. These air masses form over warm water in areas such as the Gulf of Mexico, the Caribbean Sea, and the far southern Pacific Ocean. Along with very warm weather, maritime tropical air masses can also bring heavy thunderstorms.

Air masses do not follow a strict path. Often, these huge masses bump into each other. As you know, different types

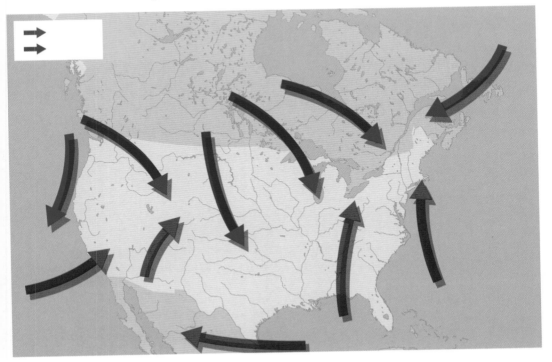

▲ Large, constantly moving air masses exist all over Earth. When two air masses collide, storms are often the result. This map shows the five main air masses that affect the weather in North America.

of air masses have different tempera-tures, humidity levels, and atmospheric pressures. So when air masses collide, they do not blend into each other. The boundary where two air masses meet is called a front. The differences in the air masses can cause dramatic changes in weather along a front.

Fronts

A front is named after the type of air mass that is moving into an area, not the mass that is already there. For example, a warm air mass may be sitting above your area. If a cold front moves in, it will have dense, cold air at its edge. This cold air pushes the warm air in front of it away. As the warm air rises, it cools. If the warm air is also moist, water vapor will condense into clouds. If all this happens quickly enough, severe thunderstorms could be the result. Most cold fronts

move through an area in a short amount of time. Once the cold front passes, the weather will usually be cooler. The atmospheric pressure will also be higher, so the skies are likely to be clear.

A warm front usually moves more slowly than a cold front. The weather along the front might bring stratus clouds. Light rain or snow may also fall. Once a warm front passes, the weather will usually be warmer, with lower atmo-spheric pressure.

Sometimes, two air masses meet along a front, and neither front moves. This is called a stationary, or nonmoving, front. In this case, the weather along the front does not really change. Once the front starts to move, however, then weather changes are in store.

Severe Weather

What pictures enter your mind when you

Reading a Weather Map

You have probably seen a weather fore-caster on television pointing to a map of the United States. Perhaps you noticed the curved lines and odd-looking triangles and half-circles that are drawn on the map. Meteorologists use these symbols to show where different fronts are located at any particular time. Triangles along a line represent a cold front. The triangles point in the direction the front is moving. Half-circles represent a warm front. As the triangles do for the cold front, the half-circles point in the direction the warm front is moving. So how do they show a stationary front? They use triangles on one side and half-circles on the other.

think of the word *storm*? Some people imagine booming thunder, lightning, and rain. Other people picture winds so strong that they bend trees in half. Still others see a dark cloud on the horizon that looks like a giant funnel. Whatever image the word *storm* conjures up for you, a storm is almost always a powerful and dramatic event. There are many different types of storms but they all result from a fierce change in the weather. Because the changes are fierce, some storms can be particularly dangerous.

Thunderstorms

Thunderstorms include three things: thunder, lightning, and rain. In dry thunderstorms, the rain does not reach the ground. Cumulonimbus clouds are the source of thunderstorms. These clouds form when warm air pushes up against a cold front. As the warm air rises, it cools and becomes denser. This leads to the formation of equally dense clouds. Eventually, rain and sometimes hail fall from these clouds with a force that can be frightening. Lightning is a spark, or energy discharge. During thunderstorms, positive and negative electrical charges build in the clouds. What looks like a jagged line of light is actually these electrical charges jumping from place to place within the clouds. These charges also jump from the clouds to the ground. Lightning is true electrical energy. As such, it carries a very strong shock. This shock is strong enough to harm or even kill people and animals. In the United

▲ As lightning bolts strike, electricity flows between the cloud and the ground. The intense electrical energy heats up the air, causing it to expand rapidly. As it expands, it creates a loud noise we hear as thunder.

States, lightning kills about 80 people each year. Lightning can also damage buildings. Each year, thousands of forest fires are caused by lightning strikes.

Thunder is a result of lightning. A bolt of lightning heats up the air around it. The air can get hotter than the surface of the Sun. Air that has heated so quickly expands with the force of an explosion. The boom of thunder is the sound of the explosion. Light travels faster than sound, so you always see lightning before you hear the thunder it causes.

Tornadoes

The weather conditions that cause thunderstorms can also cause tornadoes. A tornado is a spinning, funnel-shaped column of air that comes out of a storm cloud and touches Earth's surface. Tornadoes are one of the most destructive types of storm. They are more common in the United States than anywhere else in the world. The Great Plains

▼ The funnel-shaped column of a tornado may signal winds strong enough to uproot trees and tear the roofs off houses.

Staying Safe During Thunderstorms

Thunderstorms and lightning are severe weather events. You cannot do anything to stop the event, but you CAN do something to get through the event safely.

If you are caught outside during a thunderstorm:

• avoid touching any type of metal object that could pass the lightning's electricity to your body

• find a low area away from trees or fences

• crouch and keep your head down so you are not the tallest thing in an open field

• if you are swimming or in a boat, head for shore and find shelter away from the water.

If you are inside during a thunderstorm:

• avoid touching any kind of electrical appliance including telephones (this includes cell phones and cordless phones)

• avoid touching metal plumbing that can conduct electricity into the house.

If you are in a car with a hard top during a thunderstorm:

• try not to touch any metal inside the car. Any electrical charge will move along the outside metal skin of the car and then head toward the ground. It is safer to stay inside the car than get out of it.

Staying Safe During Tornadoes

Tornadoes are powerful storms that can be deadly. Knowing what to do if a tornado strikes can keep you safe.

Tornado Watch: this means tornadoes are possible for your area.

Tornado Warning: this means a tornado has been seen on radar or in the sky.

Many tornado warnings include a siren or an alarm. If you hear a siren or alarm, move to a safe place. DO NOT WAIT TO SEE THE TORNADO.

If you are in a building that has a basement:

• move down to the basement

• stay away from any windows.

If the building you are in does not have a basement:

• move to the center of the first or ground floor

• stay away from doors and windows

• lie on the floor under a large table or some other piece of sturdy furniture.

If you are outdoors, in an automobile, or in a mobile home:

• go immediately to a regular building or lie flat in a ditch.

states of Kansas, Nebraska, and parts of Oklahoma and Texas are considered to be in "Tornado Alley." This is because the weather patterns there make it easy for tornadoes to form.

In the United States, tornadoes most often form when a warm, moist air mass moves north from the Gulf of Mexico and reaches into the lower part of the Great Plains. This warm, moist air mass runs up against a cold, dry air mass coming from the north. All along this front, a line of heavy thunderstorms is likely to form. This line of thunderstorms can result in a line of tornadoes touching down all at once.

Tornadoes are dangerous because of the huge force of the winds they create and the objects they pick up. The worst tornadoes produce winds up to 260 miles (419 km) per hour. The atmospheric pressure inside a tornado is lower than it is on the outside of the tornado. This acts like a huge vacuum cleaner, sucking up dirt, loose wood, rocks, and other objects. Tornadoes have picked up automobiles and dropped them again several miles away. The picking up and flinging of such objects increases the danger of being in the path of a tornado.

Hurricanes

The most powerful storm on earth is a hurricane. Hurricanes are violent tropical storms with winds that blow at speeds of at least 74 miles (120 km) per hour. Hurricanes can blow at speeds of almost 200 miles (320 km) per hour. They form in warm, wet areas, usually over the ocean in tropical areas near the equator. The warm, moist air over the ocean rises and forms clouds. As the warm air rises, an area of low pressure forms and winds drive in. While the storm is taking place, there are areas of extremely high winds and torrential rain. Hurricanes can last for days and commonly stretch about 370 miles (600 km) across. When hurricanes hit land they can cause much damage, destroying buildings and ripping trees out of the ground.

▲ Hurricanes form in warm, wet conditions near the equator. As moist, warm air rises over the sea, winds rush in to replace it, causing violent storms.

You may have heard the phrase "eye of the storm." The phrase refers to the center of a hurricane. In the eye of a hurricane, the winds are calmer. Often the sky is clear. The quiet, however, does not last because the eye moves on, and the rest of the hurricane is right behind it.

A hurricane gets its energy from the ocean surface over which it forms. Once

▲ This picture shows a hurricane from space. You can see the clouds swirling around the eye of the storm.

it reaches land, it no longer has the same moist air that helped it form in the first place. Over several days, the hurricane slowly loses force. The winds begin to lessen, even though the rain may continue for a week or more.

Hurricane Katrina

In August 2005, a medium-sized hurricane formed in the Atlantic Ocean off the coast of Florida. Hurricanes are common in Florida, so no one expected this one to be anything unusual. The hurricane was named Katrina. After it passed through southern Florida and into the Gulf of Mexico, it kept growing. By the time it hit the coastlines of Louisiana, Alabama, and Mississippi, Katrina had grown to a Category 5 hurricane—the strongest there is. Water and wind slammed into the city of New Orleans in Louisiana. The banks of the rivers overflowed, the structure of several canals failed, and 80 percent of the city became flooded. At least 1,500 people also lost their lives. After nine days, Katrina finally faded away. The hurricane left an estimated $75 billion in damage to New Orleans and other cities such as Biloxi, Mississippi, and Mobile, Alabama. The destruction was so great that it drove lawmakers to make changes to prepare better for future hurricanes.

▼ When Katrina reached New Orleans it had become one of the worst hurricanes ever recorded in the Gulf of Mexico. Thousands of people lost their homes and belongings.

Frostbite and Hypothermia

Cold weather and winter storms pose particular dangers to health. If you live in a cold climate, you have probably experienced your ears being so cold you can barely feel them. Loss of feeling is the first sign of frostbite. The second sign is that the skin begins to turn white. Frostbite is damage to body tissue that results when the tissue freezes. In most cases, frostbite affects the ears, nose, fingers, or toes. Frostbite is treated by slowly warming up the "frozen" area and getting medical help. In very cold weather, people are also at risk of developing hypothermia. This condition occurs when a person's body temperature drops significantly below normal, to 95°F (35°C) or below. A person suffering from hypothermia will shiver, feel very sleepy, have trouble speaking, and feel dizzy. Hypothermia is a very serious medical condition. If you experience the signs of hypothermia yourself, or you are with someone who has them, get medical help right away.

Snowstorms and Ice

In the northern part of the United States, winter precipitation usually means snow. When moist air cools below the freezing point of water (32°F/0°C), snow falls out of the clouds instead of rain. A heavy snowstorm can cause a great deal of trouble. Snow builds up on roadways and sidewalks. This is more than an inconvenience. Blocked roadways mean that ambulances and fire vehicles cannot get to emergencies. If temperatures drop enough, water pipes in houses, schools, and businesses can freeze and burst.

When heavy snowfall and high winds occur at the same time, snowstorms create a real danger. Wind can blow snow sideways or pick it up from the ground

▲ Heavy snowfall can make objects difficult to see. Snow on roadways makes driving, and even walking, dangerous.

and keep it up in the air. In either case, it is very difficult to see. The wind also means that a person out in a storm would quickly lose body heat. It is very important if you are caught outside in a snowstorm to find shelter out of the wind. It is also important to keep your clothing as dry as possible and to cover as much of your skin as you can.

El Niño and La Niña

El Niño is the name given to a pattern of extreme weather caused by an abnormal warming of ocean waters in the eastern Pacific Ocean. It happens at least twice every ten years.

Under normal conditions in the tropical Pacific Ocean, surface winds blowing from the high-pressure region in the east to the lower pressure region in the west move ocean currents from east to west. These currents carry warm water from the coast of South America out into the Pacific Ocean toward Indonesia. As the warm surface water moves away toward the west, colder water rises to the surface. This water contains the nutrients that support many types of sea life.

In certain years, the pressure in the east is low and high in the west. The tropical winds in the east are weak. They are replaced by winds that blow from west to east. This causes the warm surface water to also move from west to east, bringing heavy rain and storms to the coast of South America. The change in the wind and current is called El Niño.

El Niño events are a threat to ocean life. They prevent the warm surface water from being replaced by the colder, nutrient-rich water. Without food, many fish die or leave the area in search of food. People who depend on fishing for their livelihood are left without fish to catch. El Niño events also affect global weather patterns. For example, areas that are normally very dry may get heavy rainfall. This may cause dangerous flooding. Other areas that normally have wet weather will face drought. This may result in brush fires that destroy millions of acres of trees.

An El Niño event is often followed by a La Niña event. The effects of a La Niña event are opposite to those of an El Niño event. A La Niña event is an unusual cooling of the ocean in the eastern tropical Pacific. During La Niña, abnormally strong winds blowing from east to west blow warm surface water toward Indonesia. Near the coast of South America, cold water rises to take the place of the warm water that is moving away. During La Niña events, there are frequent tropical storms over the warm waters of the western Pacific.

El Niño events can have an impact on the weather far away from the tropical

▼ Heavy rainfall during El Niño years can cause severe flooding. In 1981 to 1982, heavy flooding on the west coast of the United States washed out a main highway in California. The residents of the city of Half Moon Bay, near San Francisco, were stranded until the road was repaired.

▲ El Niño events can bring hotter and drier weather than usual to Indonesia, Australia, and Central America. This can cause drought and has been linked to forest fires, such as this fire in the Amazon rain forest, which burned for more than two months in 1998, destroying many thousands of acres of trees.

Pacific. For example, during an El Niño year, there may be a significant increase in rainfall and a risk of flooding in southern parts of the United States. During an El Niño year, temperatures in the winter are warmer than usual in the north central United States, and cooler than normal in the southeast and the southwest. During a La Niña year, winter temperatures are warmer than normal in the southeast, and cooler than normal in the northwest.

5 CLIMATE ZONES AND REGIONS

Climate is the normal, or regular, weather pattern for a specific area over a long period of time. An area's climate is affected by factors such as latitude, altitude, distance from the ocean, and levels of precipitation.

Latitude and Temperature

As you know, the Sun does not heat Earth evenly. This uneven heating has a direct effect on the average temperature in a particular area. Because the Sun's rays reach Earth most directly at the equator, temperatures are highest in this region. At the North and South Poles, the Sun's energy is spread over a larger area, so temperatures are lower.

Latitude is a measure of distance from the equator along imaginary lines around the world. These lines run from east to west. Distance from the equator is measured in degrees. Since the equator runs around the globe halfway between the North and South Poles, latitudes are measured either north or south of the equator. They are called north or south latitudes. There are three main climate zones on Earth. These zones are determined by their latitude.

The tropical zone is the area closest to the equator. This zone covers the area between 23.5° north latitude and 23.5° south latitude. The tropical zone receives most of the Sun's energy all year round. This means that temperatures in the tropical zone are warm.

The polar zones cover an area from 66.5° to 90° in both the Northern and Southern Hemispheres. These zones receive the least amount of the Sun's energy, so they have cold temperatures.

The temperate zones lie between the tropical and polar zones. Temperate zones run from about 23.5° to 66.5° in both the Northern and Southern Hemispheres. In these zones, the climate is neither always warm nor always cold. In the summer, more of the Sun's energy reaches Earth than in the winter. Therefore, the summers in the temperate zones are warm or hot, and the winters in the temperate zones are cold.

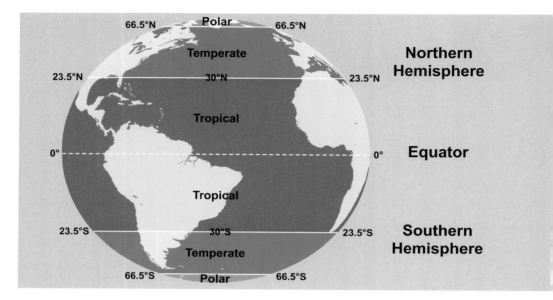

▲ Areas around the world can be divided into three main climate zones: polar, temperate, and tropical The most important factor in determining an area's temperature is its latitude. Other factors such as altitude and distance from the ocean are also important in determining the climate of a particular area.

Altitude

The height or altitude of an area can also affect its long-term climate. Mountain regions have different climates from surrounding lower areas. Temperatures in mountain areas can be very cold. This is because the higher in the troposphere you travel, the lower the temperature. Certain parts of Arizona are hot and dry all year round. High up in the mountains of Arizona, however, it is much colder.

Distance from the Ocean

An area's climate is also affected by how close it is to the ocean. Areas that are close to the ocean will have fewer extremes of temperature throughout the year than areas farther away. This is because winds from the ocean keep the temperatures fairly even. An area such as the Midwest does not have even temperatures like those in San Francisco, California. Areas in the center of North America have more extreme temperatures as part of their climate.

Precipitation

An area that sees a great deal of rain or snow each year has a different climate from an area that sees almost none. The amount of precipitation an area gets depends on whether or not there are mountains close by. It also depends on the prevailing winds.

Winds push air masses in one direction or another. Prevailing winds, like the air masses they push, can hold different amounts of water vapor. Some prevailing winds blow across dry desert areas. These winds have little moisture. Other

The Seasons

Do the seasons change at the equator? The answer is: not very much. Seasons are the result of Earth's being tilted at an angle to the Sun. As Earth travels around the Sun, different parts of Earth are warmed by different amounts. When one hemisphere is tilted toward the Sun, it receives more heat energy than the other hemisphere. It is summer in the hemisphere that is tilted toward the Sun and winter in the hemisphere that is tilted away. The tilt of Earth's axis is such that the Sun stays pretty much in the same position in relation to the equator throughout the year. The position may change by a few degrees, but that is not enough to create a definite change in season.

In the diagram below, the equator is shown as a blue line encircling each picture of Earth. As you can see, the Sun is almost always at the same angle to the equator whether it is December or June. For this reason, the equator does not really experience distinct seasons. The greatest variation in seasons comes in the temperate zones. This is because the angle of the Sun compared to Earth changes throughout the year.

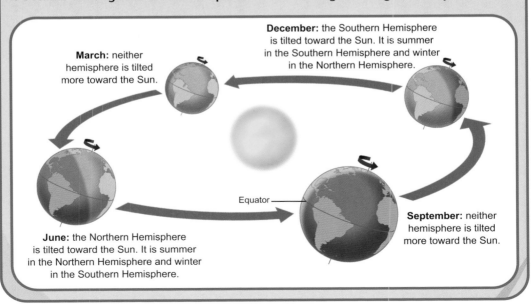

March: neither hemisphere is tilted more toward the Sun.

December: the Southern Hemisphere is tilted toward the Sun. It is summer in the Southern Hemisphere and winter in the Northern Hemisphere.

Equator

June: the Northern Hemisphere is tilted toward the Sun. It is summer in the Northern Hemisphere and winter in the Southern Hemisphere.

September: neither hemisphere is tilted more toward the Sun.

prevailing winds blow in from the oceans. These winds carry much more water vapor and, therefore, precipitation than dry inland winds.

The movement of prevailing winds can be halted by mountain ranges. When the movement of a prevailing wind that carries water vapor is halted by a mountain range, the precipitation is also halted. An example of the effect a mountain range can have on an area's climate can be seen in the state of Washington. Prevailing winds blow in from the Pacific Ocean bringing precipitation. The area on the side of the Cascade Mountains hit by the prevailing winds gets steady precipitation throughout the year. The area on the other side of the Cascade Mountains has very little precipitation. This is because the Cascade Mountains stop the movement of the prevailing winds and the precipitation.

Climate Regions

Within the three main climate zones, there are five climate regions. The world's climate regions, like climate zones, are determined by their temperature and their levels of precipitation. The world's five climate regions are tropical rainy, dry, temperate maritime, temperate continental, and polar.

If you have ever seen a picture of the Amazon rain forest, you will have seen a picture of a tropical rainy climate. The tropical rainy climate is hot and humid. Rain falls year round, nearly every day. In a tropical rainy climate at least 2 inches (5 cm) of rain falls each month. The temperatures are very warm all year round as well—above 64°F (18°C).

▲ In a tropical rain forest, year-round warm temperatures and abundant rainfall make it a good habitat for a large variety of plants and animals.

A dry climate region is one where there is very little, or no, precipitation. In fact, in many dry climate regions, more water evaporates than actually falls as rain or snow. In these areas, precipitation is usually less than 10 inches (25 cm) in an entire year. Dry climates can have either hot or cold temperatures.

A temperate maritime climate describes areas that are close to oceans, have mild winters, and high levels of precipitation. The Pacific Northwest coast of North America is an example of an area that has a temperate maritime climate. The southeastern coast of North America, which includes Florida, also has a temperate maritime climate. In this climate region, winter temperatures can be between about 27°F (–3°C) and 64°F (18°C).

Regions with temperate continental climates are far inland and away from the ocean breezes that keep temperatures fairly steady. Winters can be cold, with temperatures at 27°F (–3°C) or lower. Summers are warm and humid. In the United States, the northern Midwestern states of Wisconsin, Illinois, and Michigan are examples of places with temperate continental climates.

Regions around the North and South Poles have polar climates. The polar climate is the coldest region. Temperatures during the long winter in polar regions are always at or below freezing, which is 32°F (0°C). The average winter temperature in the Arctic is –22°F (–30°C).

▲ As well as having thick fur coats, polar bears have a layer of fat under their skin to help them keep warm in the bitterly cold temperatures of the Arctic.

Polar regions such as Antarctica have fierce cold winds that whip across frozen fields of ice. The coldest temperature that has ever been recorded on Earth was in Antarctica: –126°F (–88°C)! Temperatures in some areas in the polar regions can reach around 50°F (10°C) in the summer. In some areas around the Arctic Circle it gets warm enough to grow certain vegetables.

▲ In a temperate climate, the cooler temperatures of autumn cause the leaves on certain trees to change color.

6 CLIMATE CHANGE

Earth's climate has been through many changes at different times in its history. Some kinds of climate change are very gradual, taking place over millions of years. Some of Earth's climate changes may have been caused by changes in Earth's orbit around the Sun. Climate changes may also have been caused by the movement of continents over time. Today, there is concern that climates all over the world might be changing because of human activities that may be causing global warming.

Changes in Earth's Orbit

Some scientists believe that every 26,000 years there is a change in the shape of Earth's orbit around the Sun. The change takes place gradually over that period of time. In the present day, the Sun is closest to Earth in January. According to this hypothesis, over the 26,000 years Earth's path would change so that the Sun would be closest to Earth in July. Some scientists believe that changes in Earth's orbit around the Sun

were the cause of past ice ages. Changes in the orbit might have reduced the amount of sunlight Earth received, resulting in a cooling of the climate.

Ice Ages

Ice ages are periods lasting thousands of years, during which huge masses of ice called glaciers cover much of Earth's surface. Scientists believe that there have been at least four separate ice ages. Each one lasted for at least 100,000 years. The most recent ice age ended about 10,500 years ago.

▲ During past ice ages, huge glaciers like this one in Patagonia, Argentina, covered most of Earth's surface.

Continental Drift

The theory of continental drift states that, at one time, all the continents were joined in one giant landmass, called Pangaea. This landmass began to break apart and smaller continents were formed, which gradually drifted into their present-day positions. As the position of the continents changed, their climates changed. For example, Africa was once farther south, close to the South Pole. As it moved closer to the equator, its climate became warmer.

Changes to the Ozone Layer

The ozone layer in the stratosphere protects Earth from the Sun's harmful ultraviolet radiation. This type of radiation can cause eye damage and skin cancers. In the 1970s, scientists discovered gaps, or holes, in the ozone layer. They believed the holes were caused by chemicals that humans had released into the atmosphere. These chemicals were a special type called chlorofluorocarbons (CFCs). CFCs were used in air conditioners and refrigerators. They were also used in some spray cans. By the end of the 1970s, the United States and other countries had banned the use of CFCs. In 1992, other countries joined in the effort to protect the ozone layer that protects all of us.

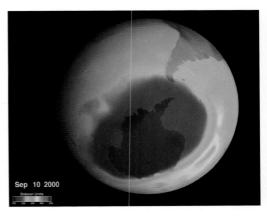

Sep 10 2000
Dobson Units

▲ The dark blue area in this picture is the thinning ozone layer located above the continent of Antarctica.

Greenhouse Effect

Gases in Earth's atmosphere hold enough heat from the Sun to support life on our planet. The gases act in much the same way as the glass of a greenhouse does. In a greenhouse, the Sun's radiation enters through glass panels. The Sun's energy warms the air inside the greenhouse and the glass traps the heat keeping the greenhouse warmer than the air outside. Gases in Earth's atmosphere, such as carbon dioxide, methane, and water vapor, act in the same way as the glass panels of a greenhouse. These gases allow radiation from the Sun to pass through and warm Earth's surface. The surface then returns some of that heat back into the air. Greenhouse gases prevent most of the heat escaping from the atmosphere.

Greenhouse gases are a natural part of Earth's atmosphere. The more there are of these gases, however, the warmer Earth's atmosphere becomes.

Human activities seem to be increasing the amount of greenhouse gases present in our atmosphere. Carbon dioxide levels are steadily increasing. The extra carbon dioxide in the atmosphere is caused by the burning of large amounts of fossil fuels, such as coal and oil. Burning wood also releases carbon dioxide into the atmosphere. Many forests have been cut down and burned to clear land for farming.

Greenhouse Gases and Weather

If the amount of greenhouse gases in the atmosphere increases, the amount of heat held in the atmosphere will also increase. This may result in changes in weather around the world because of rising temperatures and changing levels of precipitation. At first, it might sound good that Earth might get warmer. Areas where it is now too cold to grow crops

▼ Earth's surface absorbs some of the Sun's heat energy and returns some of it back into the atmosphere. Some of the heat is trapped by greenhouse gases. The more greenhouse gases in the atmosphere, the more heat is trapped.

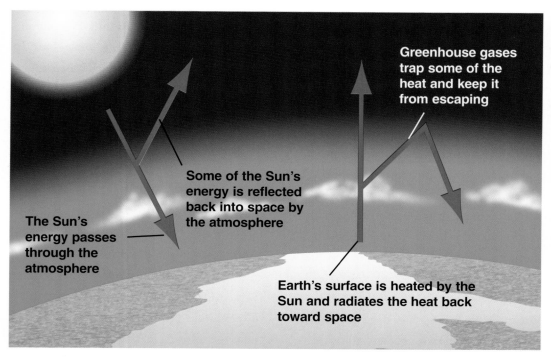

Greenhouse gases trap some of the heat and keep it from escaping

Some of the Sun's energy is reflected back into space by the atmosphere

The Sun's energy passes through the atmosphere

Earth's surface is heated by the Sun and radiates the heat back toward space

could become important agricultural centers. More of the world's people could be fed if there were more farmland. If temperatures were higher, however, water in the soil would evaporate more quickly.

▲ Higher global temperatures can cause farmland and lake beds to dry out like this land in Australia.

This may result in good farmland being turned into dry dust. Warmer temperatures in the atmosphere would also mean warmer ocean temperatures. This might lead to more hurricanes worldwide.

Earth's atmosphere, weather, and climates work together in a type of balanced system. As we learn more about the different causes of the weather that affects each of us, we also learn that we are a part of the balance as well.

Global Warming

Over the last 125 years, the average temperature of Earth's troposphere has increased by about 0.9°F (0.5°C). This increase in temperature could have serious consequences. Even if Earth's temperatures rise by only a small amount, the increase could melt some of the ice at the North and South Poles. If this happens, ocean levels would rise all over the world. This could lead to many large cities ending up under water. Many scientists believe that the warming trend is partly due to human activity. Some scientists, however, believe that the warming trend is just part of a natural cycle. Others think it may be the result of a combination of human activity and natural factors.

▲ Burning fossil fuels for electricity releases large amounts of carbon dioxide into the atmosphere. Greenhouse gases such as carbon dioxide contribute to the problem of global warming.

GLOSSARY

air mass A large body of air with the same temperature and humidity

altitude The height of an area above sea level

atmosphere A layer of gases around a planet such as Earth

atmospheric pressure The downward pressure at any point on Earth's surface caused by the weight of the air above

cirrus A wispy type of cloud that resembles a curl of hair

continental Relating to a large landmass; a continental air mass forms over land; a continental climate is relatively dry, with hot summers and cold winters

continental drift The theory that Earth's continents once formed a great landmass that later broke apart into smaller landmasses, which drifted into the current position of the continents

convection The way heat energy is transferred through liquids or gases

convection current The constant rising and sinking of warm and cold air resulting in continuous movement

Coriolis effect The swerve in the winds caused by Earth's rotation

cumulonimbus A combination cloud formed from cumulus and nimbus clouds; cumulonimbus clouds often indicate that precipitation is on its way

cumulus White, fluffy clouds

density Amount of air or water molecules in a certain amount of air

electromagnetic radiation Energy transfer in the form of electric and magnetic waves

evaporation The process by which water molecules escape into the air as water vapor

fog A cloud that forms close to the ground when relative humidity is 100 percent at ground level

front The boundary between two air masses with different temperatures and levels of humidity

global warming A steady increase in the average temperature around the world

global winds Winds that blow from certain directions and travel long distances

hurricane A violent tropical storm with winds that blow at least 74 miles (120 km) per hour

ice age Period lasting thousands of years during which glaciers covered much of Earth's surface

latitude A measure of distance from the equator along imaginary lines that run east to west around the world; imaginary lines north of the equator are called north latitudes; imaginary lines south of the equator are called south latitudes

local winds Winds that blow over a small area or over a short distance

maritime Having to do with the sea; maritime air masses form over the oceans.

mass A measure of the amount of matter something contains

mesosphere The layer of Earth's atmosphere located above the stratosphere

meteorologist A weather scientist

nimbostratus A cloud that combines nimbus and stratus clouds

nimbus A cloud that produces precipitation

ozone A gas in the atmosphere that absorbs harmful radiation from the Sun and prevents it from reaching Earth

polar regions Areas around the North and South Poles with very cold temperatures

precipitation Any form of water from a cloud that reaches Earth's surface

prevailing winds The winds that blow most frequently in a particular direction over an area

radiation Energy from the Sun

stratosphere The layer of the atmosphere located above the troposphere

stratus A cloud that forms in flat, gray layers

temperate zones Climate zones that run between about 23.5° to 66.5° latitude in both the Northern and Southern Hemispheres, with temperatures that vary with the seasons

thermosphere The layer of the atmosphere farthest away from Earth's surface and closest to the Sun

tornado Spinning, funnel-shaped column of air that comes out of a storm cloud and touches Earth's surface

tropical zone climate zone closest to the equator, which ranges between 23.5° north latitude and 23.5° south latitude and has warm temperatures all year round

troposphere The layer of the atmosphere closest to Earth's surface; the troposphere contains most of the gases in the atmosphere

water cycle The natural process by which water is constantly recycled between Earth's surface, the atmosphere, and living things

water vapor Water in the form of a gas

wind-chill factor The effect of wind combined with cold temperatures that take away body heat

FURTHER INFORMATION

Books
Potter, Tony. *Weather.* BBC Fact Finders (series). Parkwest Publications, 1990.

Silverstein, Alvin. *Weather and Climate.* Science Concepts (series). 21st Century, 1998.

Varilla, Mary (ed.). *Scholastic Atlas of Weather.* Scholastic, Inc., 2004.

Web Sites
Nature Watch
www.enature.com/articles/detail.asp?storyID=589

Making a Weather Station
www.miamisci.org/hurricane/weatherstation.html

SciJinks Weather Laboratory
scijinks.jpl.nasa.gov/weather/

DVDs
Inside Hurricane Katrina. National Geographic, 2005.

The Weather. BBC, 2003.

INDEX